Marmaduke's
Phonics

Marmaduke's Alphabet

Karen Bryant-Mole

Evans

Marmaduke's Phonics

- **Blends at the Beginning** • **Letters at the End**
- **Marmaduke Plays I-Spy** • **Marmaduke's Alphabet**
- **Marmaduke's Rhymes** • **Three Sounds, One Word**

Published by Evans Brothers Limited
2A Portman Mansions
Chiltern Street
London W1M 1LE

© BryantMole Books 1999

First published in 1999

Printed in Spain by G. Z. Printek

British Library Cataloguing in Publication Data

Bryant-Mole, Karen
  Alphabet. - (Marmaduke's Phonics)
  1.English language - Alphabet - Pictorial works - Juvenile literature
  I.Title
  421.1

  ISBN 0237521113

The name **Marmaduke** is a registered trade mark.

Created by Karen Bryant-Mole
Photographed by Zul Mukhida
Designed by Jean Wheeler
Teddy bear by Merrythought Ltd

About this book

Marmaduke the bear helps children to understand phonics by guiding them through the learning process in a fun, friendly way.

This book introduces children to the idea that written letters of the alphabet represent sounds. Children are shown a letter and then told that it makes the sound that is heard at the beginning of a particular word. The sounds made by the letter combinations 'ch', 'sh' and 'th' are also introduced.

* Remember to use the letter sounds rather than their names. The word 'alligator' starts with the sound 'a' not the name 'ay'.

contents

a

a is for **alligator**

Marmaduke is admiring the alligator.

b c

b

b is for
butterfly
and **c** is for
camera

c

What a beautiful butterfly!
Marmaduke will go 'click' with his camera.

d e

d is for **dinosaur** and e is for **egg**

Marmaduke thinks dinosaurs are delightful.
Be extra careful with that egg, Marmaduke!

f

f is for **fish**

f

Marmaduke wants to make friends
with this fish.

g h

g is for **guitar** and **h** is for **horse**

g

h

Marmaduke is good at playing the guitar. The music makes the horse happy.

i

i is for **insect**

Marmaduke thinks insects are interesting.

j k

j is for **jam**
and **k** is for
kangaroo

j

k

Marmaduke's jam
is in a jar.
The kangaroo is
keen to try some.

l

l is for **lollipop**

Marmaduke
likes to lick
his lollipop.

m   n

m

n

m is for
mirror and **n** is
for **necklace**

Can you see Marmaduke in the mirror?
Nice necklace, Marmaduke!

o

o is for **octopus**

This octopus often visits Marmaduke.

13

p q

p is for **pyjamas** and **q** is for **quilt**

Marmaduke is wearing a pair of pyjamas.
Soon he will sleep quietly under his quilt.

r

r is for **rocket**

r

Marmaduke's rocket is red.

s t

s is for **sand** and t is for **tortoise**

Marmaduke is sitting in some sand.
The tortoise is waiting for his turn.

u

u

u is for **umbrella**

Marmaduke is sitting under an umbrella.

v w

v is for **vegetables** and **w** is for **watch**

Marmaduke has a variety of vegetables.
His watch tells him when it is dinner time!

X

box ends in x

Can you see a six on Marmaduke's toy box?

Y

y is for yo-yo

Marmaduke is playing with his yellow yo-yo.

z

z is for **zebra**

Some zebras live in zoos.

two letters, one sound

ch

ch is for **chocolate** and **sh** is for **sheep**

sh

Marmaduke has a big chunk of chocolate.
He is going to share it with the sheep.

th is for **thermometer**

Thank you for showing us your thermometer, Marmaduke!

index